CONGRATULATIONS

Ellyn Sanna

BARBOUR
PUBLISHING, INC.

Published by Barbour Publishing, Inc., P.O. Box 719, Uhrichsville, Ohio 44683 http://www.barbourbooks.com

 Member of the
Evangelical Christian
Publishers Association

Printed in China.

Contents

1. Welcome!. 6

2. An Awesome Responsibility 11

3. Smiles and Laughter. 16

4. Sleepless Nights, Exhausting Days 21

5. Marriage and Babies. 26

6. Messages from God 31

7. Always Your Baby—and Always God's 36

Welcome!

A woman giving birth to a child has pain because her time has come;
but when her baby is born she forgets the anguish
because of her joy that a child is born into the world.
—John 16:21 (NIV)

Date of birth: _____

Time: _____

Baby's weight:_____

Length: _____

Where did you come from, baby dear?
Out of the everywhere into here.

If you're a new parent, be prepared

- . . .to feel like you're in love.
- . . .to spend most of your baby's first month just looking at him or her.
- . . .to think everything about your baby is lovely and amazing: her tiny hands and feet; the way she yawns; the shape of her mouth when she's sleeping; the small, contented noises she makes when she eats.
- . . .to cry the first time he gets his shots.
- . . .for total strangers to touch and talk to your baby—and for them to always get her sex wrong.

Your baby's first cry is the one you hear in the delivery room,
the triumphant, tension-shattering sound that says,
"I'm here, I'm breathing, I'm alive!"
—KATHERINE KARLSRUD

 ## CONGRATULATIONS!

Childbirth ends our pregnancies, just as death will one day end this life's limitations. When that day comes, when we are born from death's darkness into a brilliance brighter than any we've ever seen, will we experience the same sense of wonder and recognition we feel at our baby's birth?

—ELLYN SANNA, *Motherhood: A Spiritual Journey*

To see what you have made coming forth from within you, and in that moment of first vision, to love it totally and for always. . . . Can anyone who has not given birth, in fact or in imagination, understand what it means for God to have created us? And will the sight of God in heaven be like this, when after unbearable pain and waiting the hidden is made known?

—MARGARET HEBBLETHWAITE, *Motherhood and God*

Now we see but a poor reflection; as in a mirror;
then we shall see face to face.
Now I know in part; then I shall know fully,
even as I am fully known.
—1 CORINTHIANS 13:12 (NIV)

O young thing, your mother's lovely armful!
How sweet the fragrance of your body!
—EURIPIDES

Dear Lord, thank You for giving me this amazing miracle—my baby. Just looking at her fills me with wonder and praise. Thank You for each tiny part of her, each fingernail and hair, each brain cell and blood vessel. I am filled with awe and love for her—and for You.

You knit me together in my mother's womb. . . .
I am fearfully and wonderfully made. . . .
My frame was not hidden from you when
I was made in the secret place.
When I was woven together in the depths of the earth,
your eyes saw my unformed body.
—PSALM 139:13–16 (NIV)

Lullaby

Golden slumbers kiss your eyes,
Smiles awake you when you rise.
Sleep, pretty baby, do not cry,
And I will sing a lullaby.

An Awesome Responsibility

I am holding you by your right hand—
I, the Lord your God—and I say to you,
Don't be afraid; I am here to help you.
—ISAIAH 41:13 (TLB)

Who visited your baby in the hospital?

_____

_____

What gifts did they bring?

_____

_____

What did your baby wear home from the hospital?

_____

I remember leaving the hospital. . .thinking, "Wait, are they going to let me just walk off with him? . . .I don't have a license to do this. [We're] *just amateurs."*

—ANNE TYLER

CONGRATULATIONS!

Except that right side up is best,
there is not much to learn about holding a baby.
There are one hundred and fifty-two distinctly different ways—
and all are right! At least all will do.
—HEYWOOD BROUN

When you're a new parent, be prepared

. . .to find that taking care of your baby is the hardest job you've ever had.
. . .to wish you could hurt in your baby's place.
. . .to wonder why you ever thought that the work for which you get paid was a hard job.
. . .to envy parents who make it look so easy.
. . .to feel more frustrated, more discouraged, and more incredibly joyful than you've ever felt before.

It is still the biggest gamble in the world. . . .
It's huge and scary—it's an act of infinite optimism.
—GILDA RADNER

My only advice is to stay aware,
listen carefully, and yell for help if you need it.
—JUDY BLUME

"Leave her alone," said Jesus.
"Why are you bothering her?
She has done a beautiful thing. . . .
She did what she could."
MARK 14:6, 8 (NIV)

Parenting a little one at best is overwhelming—overwhelming in the emotion, time, energy, and decision making it takes. Did you ever imagine that one so tiny, so longed for and sought after, could be so intrusive of every area of your life? Day or night, with no regard for people, venue, or time, the feeding, diapering, and consoling *must* take place.

. . .If you are tempted to be overwhelmed today with feelings of inadequacy, step back and remember that in spite of others' condemnation and misperception, Jesus affirmed Mary. "She has done a beautiful thing to me. . . . *She did what she could.*"

—RUTH TUTTLE CONARD
Devotions for New Moms

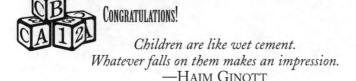# Congratulations!

Children are like wet cement.
Whatever falls on them makes an impression.
—HAIM GINOTT

New parents quickly learn that raising children is
a kind of desperate improvisation.
—BILL COSBY, *Fatherhood*

Today, God, You know I didn't feel up to this enormous job You've given me. The baby never stopped crying, it seemed, not since five o'clock this morning. I'm so tired. There's so much I should be doing, so much for which I'm responsible. I don't know how to do it all. I feel overwhelmed.

Thank You, God, for being with me. I hear Your quiet voice reminding me, "I love you, child. Remember—you are not the source of your baby's salvation. I am. Put your baby in My hands and rest now. I alone can love him perfectly—just as I love you. I will help you carry this awesome responsibility joyfully."

What a relief, dear Father, to lean on You. And what comfort to know Your angels are helping me take care of my baby.

I tell you that their angels in heaven always see
the face of my Father in heaven.
—MATTHEW 18:10 (NIV)

Lullaby

Hush, my dear, lie still and slumber,
Holy angels guard thy bed!
Heavenly blessings without number
Gently falling on thy head.

—ISAAC WATTS

Smiles and Laughter

We were filled with laughter,
and we sang for joy. . . .
Yes, the LORD has done amazing things for us!
What joy!
—PSALM 126:2–3 (NLT)

I have no name. I am but two days old.
What shall I call thee?
I happy am, Joy is my name.

Your baby's first smile: _____

Date _____ Age _____

Who your baby smiled at: _____

Your baby's first laugh: _____

Date _____ Age _____

What made your baby laugh: _____

When we hear a baby laugh, it is the loveliest thing that can happen to us.
—SIGMUND FREUD

When you're a new parent, be prepared

- . . .to find yourself falling in love all over again the first time your baby smiles at you.
- . . .to discover that blowing on your baby's tummy is the funniest thing you ever did.
- . . .to wake up one morning and hear your baby laughing out loud, all by herself in her crib.
- . . .to find yourself doing anything at all, no matter how silly or undignified, just to hear your baby laugh.
- . . .to think that playing peek-a-boo is the high point of your day.

When the first baby laughed for the first time,
the laugh broke into a thousand pieces
and they all went skipping about,
and that was the beginning of fairies.
—J. M. BARRIE, *Peter Pan*

# Congratulations!

Begin, baby boy,
to recognize your mother with a smile.
—Virgil

Babies smile from the moment they're born—but you're never really certain they smiling *at* you. "Gas bubbles," your mother and mother-in-law will tell you (although why a gas bubble should produce a smile in an infant when it doesn't later in life, I've never known). At any rate, those early smiles are fleeting, and they seem distracted, as though the baby's thoughts were turned inward to some weighty matter.

But then one day, when your baby's a month or two old, she meets your eyes and gives a wide, gummy smile of pure joy. You're startled, amazed, awed, delighted; you realize for the first time the miracle of a simple smile. A mere stretching of our facial muscles communicates so much to each other, more than any word, more than any book.

Up until now, your baby's been a solemn little person. You love her more than you thought possible, and she's so close to you that she's almost inside your skin. But when she studied your face with her bright intent eyes, you were never quite sure what she was thinking. All these weeks you've been stumbling around in exhaustion, caring for this infinitely beloved little person who could express her appreciation only by ceasing to cry—but now she's rewarded you with this amazing smile.

She looks as surprised and delighted as you feel, as though she

suddenly got the punch line of a joke she's been hearing for weeks. Her smile pulls you close to her in a way you haven't yet experienced. You find yourself totally engaged with her personhood, the unique individual she is.

What is overpowering is simply the fact that a baby is life. It is also a mess, but such an appealing one that we look past the mess to the jewel underneath.

—BILL COSBY, *Fatherhood*

Dear Lord, thank You so much for my baby's smiles. Her laughter fills me with joy. She is so precious to me, God. I don't have enough words to express my love and gratitude. All I can say is thank You.

Lullaby

You are my sunshine, my little sunshine.
You make me happy when skies are gray.
You'll never know, dear, how much I love you.
Please don't take my sunshine away.

Sleepless Nights, Exhausting Days

"My grace is sufficient for you,
for my power is made perfect in weakness."
—2 CORINTHIANS 12:9 (NIV)

First time your baby slept through the night:

Date _____ Age _____

A baby is
an inestimable blessing
and a bother.
—MARK TWAIN

I actually remember feeling delight, at two o'clock in the morning,
when the baby woke for his feed,
because I so longed to have another look at him.
—MARGARET DRABBLE

 CONGRATULATIONS!

When you're a new parent, be prepared

. . .to do anything to get your baby to sleep, including driving around the block twenty times at eleven o'clock at night.
. . .to wake up terrified that he's dead the first time your baby sleeps through the night.
. . .to find that greeting card and laundry soap commercials bring tears to your eyes.
. . .to wish that parenthood came with lunch breaks, vacation days, and sick time.
. . .to have the phone ring as soon as your baby falls asleep, startling him into a crying spell.
. . .to smell like sour milk a lot of the time.
. . .to find that your baby needs his diaper changed just as company walks through the door.

Having a family is like having a bowling alley installed in your brain.
—MARTIN MULL

CONGRATULATIONS!

With our first child, that first night home from the hospital was a living nightmare for me. If she snuffled, I flew to the bassinet. If she was quiet, I also flew to her side, certain that I had somehow smothered her. Oh, that I had listened to a loving husband's advice (I wrongly thought him quite callous at the time!) and remembered that we had done our best, I needed to sleep, and God was awake, watching over us all!

. . .And He never goes to sleep. When you are bending over this soft little bundle in the night to lift her, comfort her, diaper her, or feed her, remember that your heavenly Father is bending over you.

—RUTH TUTTLE CONARD
Devotions for New Moms

I lift up my eyes to the hills—
where does my help come from?
My help comes from the LORD,
the Maker of heaven and earth.
He will not let your foot slip—
he who watches over you will not slumber.
—PSALM 121:1–3 (NIV)

 CONGRATULATIONS!

There never was a child so lovely but
his mother was glad to get him asleep.
—RALPH WALDO EMERSON

Dear God, You know how much I love my baby. I'm so glad You gave him to us; I love him so much. Help me remember, Father, that one day he'll sleep through the night—and so will I again. One day I won't have to change his clothes five times a day—or mine either. One day again I'll have time to do work I enjoy, talk on the phone with a friend, read a book, or clean my house.

In the meantime, God, help me to keep my eyes fixed on You. Remind me to rely only on You for strength. I know You will see me through this joyful, exhausting time.

Babies are always more trouble than you thought—
and more wonderful.
—CHARLES OSGOOD

Lullaby

Hush-a-bye, don't you cry.
Go to sleep, my little baby.
Daddy loves you,
Mommy loves you.
And Jesus loves our little baby.

Marriage and Babies

Your baby's weight at:

One month: _____

Two months: _____

Six months: _____

Nine months: _____

One year: _____

When you have a baby, you set off an explosion in your marriage,
and when the dust settles,
your marriage is different from what it was.
Not better, necessarily; not worse, necessarily; but different.
—NORA EPHRON

When you're a new parent, be prepared
...to be too exhausted for romantic moments.
...to have the baby start to cry if you ever do feel romantic.
...to find that your baby's gastrointestinal habits have become your favorite topic of conversation.
...for seeing one movie a year in the theater—and falling asleep when you try to watch one together on the VCR.
...to call home eight times the first time you leave the baby with a baby-sitter.
...for the fact that weekends and vacations together will never be quite the same.

If you're a new mother, be prepared
...to be the one who always wakes up when the baby cries.
...to have it take longer to wake your husband up than it would to just get up and take care of the baby yourself.
...to feel a little jealous if your husband gets to escape and go off to work and you don't.

If you're a new father, be prepared
...to think your baby sleeps through the night six months before she really does.
...to have your wife hand you the baby with a desperate look on her face as soon as you walk through the door at the end of the day.
...to feel a little jealous if your wife gets to spend more time with the baby than you do.

Having a child is surely
the most beautifully irrational act that
two people in love can commit.
—BILL COSBY, *Fatherhood*

Having a baby changes your marriage forever. For at least the next eighteen or so years, the two of you will be less spontaneous, less focused on each other. The time you have for each other will be more limited, and you will be more emotionally drained when you are together, more apt to vent your frustrations on the other. But even though that's true, the fact is, this baby ties you even tighter to one another than before. No one else loves him quite as much, no one else thinks he's quite as fascinating and handsome and intelligent. This baby pulls the two of you together in a knot that can never be broken.

I begin to love this little creature, and to anticipate his birth
as a fresh twist to a knot, which I do not wish to untie.
—MARY WOLLSTONECRAFT

Love isn't how you feel.
It's what you do.
—Madeleine L'Engle

God, our baby has enriched our marriage so much—and yet she also drains our marriage, puts a strain on it that wasn't there before. Sometimes being a parent is such hard work—and being married is hard work too.

And yet in the midst of all this hard work, You give us such joy. Keep our commitment to each other strong and firm, even when we're tired and cross. Help us to support one another and forgive one another.

Thank You for our marriage, Father. May it be a strong shelter for our child, a place where Your love and joy can dwell.

Most important of all,
continue to show deep love for each other,
for love covers a multitude of sins.
—1 Peter 4:8 (NLT)

Lullaby

Hush, little baby, don't you cry,
Daddy loves you and so do I.

Messages from God

Long to grow up into the fullness of your salvation;
cry for this as a baby cries for his milk.
—1 PETER 2:3 (TLB)

Milestones

Baby's age when he or she. . .

Rolled over for the first time: _____

Ate first solid foods: _____

Sat up alone the first time: _____

Crawled for the first time: _____

Stood up: _____

Took a first step: _____

 ## Congratulations!

Think always that, having the child at your breast,
and having it in your arms, you have God's blessing there.
—ELIZABETH CLINTON

When you're a new parent, be prepared

. . .to sense God's quiet presence while you rock your baby to
sleep.
. . .to understand in a new way what it cost God to send His Son
to earth.
. . .to catch sight of God's face in the unconditional love your
child gives you.

Every child comes with the message that
God is not yet discouraged of man.
—RABINDRANATH TAGORE

"I stinky," my toddler says and holds up her arms to me, smiling confidently. I put off the moment as long as I can, I must admit, but eventually I scoop her up and lay her on the changing table. As I clean her, she chatters to me about Pooh Bear and Grandma and Daddy-at-work. I shake powder, then bend and blow on her tummy. She wiggles with delight, beaming up at me. Face to face, we smile at each other, exchange kisses, and I realize that her dirtiness was actually an opportunity for communion between us.

. . .We are to have this same attitude of confidence and love toward God. . .the same delight in His presence that our children have in ours. Even our mistakes, our selfishness and failure, can be opportunities for communion with God. . . . Our recognition of our need for God's cleansing should be as simple, as automatic, as confident as my daughter's "I stinky."

. . .God's grace is not the stern thing we always thought. Instead, it is simple and joyful as a child's love for a mother or as a mother's love for a child. We do not have to strive and labor to merit this love; it simply pours down on us, moment by moment, no matter what we're doing. It frees us from the need to achieve, to prove ourselves. Like a child rocked in a mother's arms, even asleep we are nestled in grace.

—ELLYN SANNA, *Motherhood: A Spiritual Journey*

 CONGRATULATIONS!

It is not a slight thing when they, who are fresh from God, love us.
—CHARLES DICKENS

Dear Jesus, thank You for showing me Your love through my baby. When I watch him sleeping in his crib, when I listen to his soft coos and crows of laughter, when I feel his small arms around my neck, I sense Your presence with me. Thank You for this little love letter from You to me. Accept the love and care I give to him as a love gift back to You.

As a mother comforts her child,
so will I comfort you.
—ISAIAH 66:13 (NIV)

Lullaby

Rock-a-bye baby, thy cradle is green,
Father's a nobleman, Mother's a queen.
Sister's a lady and wears a gold ring,
And Brother's a drummer, drums for the king.

Always Your Baby— and Always God's

"I am the woman who stood here that time praying to the Lord! I asked him to give me this child, and he has given me my request; and now I am giving him to the Lord for as long as he lives." So she left [the child] *there...for the Lord to use.*
—1 SAMUEL 1:26–28 (TLB)

More Milestones

Your baby's first words: _____

_____

Your baby's first-birthday guests: _____

_____

Your baby's first-birthday presents: _____

_____

What your baby did: _____

Your children are
always your "babies,"
even if they have gray hair.
—JANET LEIGH

When you're a new parent, be prepared

. . .to have your heart ache every time you and your baby are
    separated.
. . .to be a little sad as you watch your baby change so fast.
. . .to feel your heart go out to every parent whose child is in
    trouble.
. . .to lie awake worrying more than you ever did before.
. . .to wish you could somehow guarantee your child a perfect
    world.
. . .to find that the only answer to your fears lies in God.

 CONGRATULATIONS!

Suddenly I realize that the sheer intensity of my love cannot protect this child from the perils of life. Spinal meningitis. Playground tragedies. Traffic accidents. God, I cannot stand it. My chest contracts with unborn grief. My breath comes quickly. To risk love is to risk loss. Shadows stretch across the living room and across my mind. And then I hear it. The still, small voice saying gently, deep inside, "You're not a proud new owner. You're a trusted caretaker. This is My child, and I've lent him to you. Love him dearly, but hold him freely. Trust Me for the days ahead."

—SANDRA BERNLEHR CLARK
in *A Mother's Touch*

*Children are the
living messages we send to
a time we will not see.*
—JOHN W. WHITEHEAD

We can't give our children the future,
strive though we may to make it secure.
But we can give them the present.
—KATHLEEN NORRIS

Dear God, help me to put my baby in Your hands each day of her life. You are her only safety, Lord. I know You love her even more than I do, and I trust You to care for her all the days of her life, no matter what. When worries attack me, remind me to give each fear to You. Thank You for the peace You give my heart.

"Before I formed you in the womb
I knew you,
before you were born
I set you apart."
—JEREMIAH 1:5 (NIV)

Lullaby

Sleep, baby, sleep,
Thy father guards the sheep.
Thy mother shakes the dreamland tree,
And down drops pretty dreams for thee.
Sleep, baby, sleep.